T5-COB-766

REMARKS

ON SOME OF THE

CHARACTERS OF SHAKESPERE.

AMS PRESS
NEW YORK

REMARKS

ON SOME OF THE

CHARACTERS OF SHAKESPERE,

BY

THOMAS WHATELY, ESQ.

THE AUTHOR OF "OBSERVATIONS ON MODERN GARDENING."

―――― ILLE PROFECTO
REDDERE PERSONÆ SCIT CONVENIENTIA CUIQUE.
Horat.

EDITED BY

RICHARD WHATELY, D.D.

ARCHBISHOP OF DUBLIN.

THE THIRD EDITION.

LONDON:
JOHN W. PARKER, WEST STRAND.
MDCCCXXXIX.

Library of Congress Cataloging in Publication Data

Whately, Thomas, d. 1772.
    Remarks on some of the characters of Shakespeare.

    1. Shakespeare, William, 1564-1616--Characters.
2. Shakespeare, William, 1564-1616. Macbeth.
3. Shakespeare, William, 1564-1616. King Richard III.
I. Title.
PR2989.W5 1972   822.3'3   78-177827
ISBN 0-404-06917-7

Reprinted from an original copy in the collection
of the University of Illinois Library

From the edition of 1839, London
First AMS edition published in 1972
Manufactured in the United States of America

AMS PRESS INC.
NEW YORK, N. Y.   10003

PREFACE BY THE EDITOR.

The Work of which the third edition is now before the reader, was first published, after the author's death, by his brother, the late Rev. Dr. Joseph Whately, father of the present editor.

The parallel between the characters of Richard and Macbeth, was only one out of several in which the author had designed to illustrate the peculiar power of Shakespere in the delineation of character; but he suspended his design, in order to finish and prepare for the press his well-known treatise on Modern Gardening, first published in 1770. Immediately after that time he was engaged in such an active scene of public life, (being private secretary to one of the Ministers,) as left him but little leisure for literary pursuits. In 1772 he died, leaving behind him, in manuscript, the work as it now appears; which, though but a small portion of what had been originally designed, is complete as far as it goes, and was " esteemed," (says the original editor,) " by all who have perused the manuscript, as too valuable to be suppressed."*

Subsequently, this decision has been fully confirmed by competent judges; who have con-

* The late Mr. Hazlitt mentions this work with approbation; though, through some unaccountable slip of memory, he speaks of the author under the name of "*Mason.*" This mistake, though pointed out at the time in a Review, has been retained in a subsequent edition.

sidered this little volume, not only as entitled to a high rank among the commentaries on Shakespere, but as presenting some very curious and interesting views of that which the great dramatist so well delineated—human nature.

It may be proper to notice in this place a remark which I have heard made on this work, and which, though not necessarily implying any disparagement of it, may yet be so understood. It has been suggested that some of the passages brought forward by Mr. Whately as characteristic, and as appropriate, respectively, to Richard and Macbeth, were probably not meant to be such by the poet himself, but may have dropped, as it were, from his pen, casually, and without any thought of exhibiting the peculiar character of the speaker.

It should be remembered, however, that, supposing this opinion to be perfectly correct, it does not at all militate against anything that is maintained in these pages, nor in the least detract from their value. For Mr. Whately, it should be observed, is merely pointing out that such and such speeches *do* indicate character; not that they were, in each case, written with that *design*. If, then, they really *are* characteristic, the criticism is fully borne out, whatever may have been the design of Shakespere.

If I were called on to state my own conjecture as to that design, I should be disposed to go much beyond the remark above alluded to. I doubt whether Shakespere ever had any thought at all of making his personages speak characteristically. In most instances, I conceive— probably in all—he drew characters correctly, because he *could not avoid it;* and would never have attained, in that department, such excellence as he has, if he had made any studied efforts for it. And the same, probably, may be said of Homer, and of those other writers who have excelled the most in delineating characters.

A man possessing, like Shakespere, a very *vivid imagination,* combined with an insight into human nature, will, when he figures to himself (to use a homely but expressive phrase) any fictitious personage, spontaneously and unavoidably conceive it with such a force and distinctness of form and colouring, that it will stand before his mind's eye, as an individual; and the image thus framed will suggest to him every expression and action that is characteristic of the imagined individual. The speeches, consequently, which he puts into the mouth of such a personage, and the conduct he attributes to him, will necessarily be characteristic, without any distinct effort or care in each case to make them so, but merely from the vividness of the original conception.

A similar process takes place in the mind of every man of ordinary good sense, in the case of any *real* individual whom he intimately knows. We usually conjecture pretty accurately concerning a very intimate acquaintance, how he would speak or act on any supposed occasion: if any one should report to us his having done or said something quite out of character, we should at once be struck with the inconsistency; and we often represent to ourselves, and describe to others, without any conscious effort, not only the substance of what he would have been likely to say, but even his characteristic phrases and looks.

Now Shakespere's peculiar genius consisted chiefly, I conceive, in his forming the same distinct and consistent idea of an imaginary person, that an ordinary man forms of a real and well-known individual. Shakespere *could* no more have endured an expression from the lips of Macbeth inconsistent with the character originally conceived, than an ordinary man could attribute to his most respectable acquaintance the behaviour of a ruffian, or to a human Being, the voice of a bird, or to a European, the features and hue of a negro. Hence, characteristic conduct and language spontaneously suggested themselves to the great dramatist's pen. He called his personages into being, and left them, as it were, to speak and act for themselves.

I even doubt whether he was himself aware wherein his peculiar forte lay;—whether a collection of the " beauties of Shakespere," if one had been made by the poet himself, would not have omitted most of those marvellous touches of character for which we most admire him;—and whether such a volume as the present, if he could have seen it, would not, though he would have recognised its views as correct, have afforded him the amusement of a startling novelty.

Some few persons, however,—among others the celebrated Mr. Kemble,—have dissented from Mr. Whately's view of the character of Macbeth; whose courage they consider him to have underrated. But this apparent dissent seems to have arisen from a misapprehension of the critic's meaning, notwithstanding the great perspicuity with which he has written. Mr. Whately merely denies to Macbeth that *particular kind* of courage which characterizes Richard the Third. But every one must admit that Macbeth, as described in the following pages, is such a character, that every general would congratulate himself in having under his command an army, composed of men, exactly (in respect of courage) resembling him.

The truth is, however, that "courage" and other cognate terms are commonly applied by different persons, (and sometimes by the same person,) to such different qualities, or different modifications of the same quality, as to give occasion to many disputes which, on attentive examination, turn out to be merely verbal.

A question was raised, for instance, some years ago, whether Shakespere intended to represent Falstaff as a coward; the negative being maintained in an ingenious pamphlet, which some persons supposed to have been written merely in sport, by way of showing what could be advanced in favour of the most extravagant position. The author appears, however, to have been perfectly serious, and not to have differed materially in his idea of Falstaff's character, from the generality of the readers of Shakespere. He only used the term "coward" in a more restricted sense. Shakespere's Falstaff, though deliberately preferring disgrace to imminent danger, is clearly a character of constitutional coolness and presence of mind. His cowardice, if it is to be so called, is altogether a contrast to that (for instance) of Sir Andrew Aguecheek. In his encounter with Douglas, the device to which he resorts is equally inconsistent with the character either of a man of chivalrous valour, or of one paralysed by fright.

On the different varieties of courage and of timidity, and on other points connected with the subject of this volume, there are some admirable remarks in several passages of a series of articles on Sir Walter Scott's Romances, which appeared in the Quarterly Review, and in the London Review of 1829. These articles are by the same hand; and as they are among the most valuable critical works in this, or perhaps in any language, I have taken the liberty of extracting and subjoining, in an Appendix, the passages alluded to.

I cannot conclude without expressing a wish that the author of those articles, or some other similarly gifted writer, would employ some of his leisure hours in carrying on the illustration of Shakespere, designed and commenced by Mr. Whately. Several of the characters of the great dramatist—comic, as well as tragic,—afford materials for such parallels as that between Richard and Macbeth.

In these days, when every department of nature is scrutinized by men of eminent talents, and when the minutest researches, for instance of the anatomist and the physiologist, into things seemingly insignificant, are often found to lead to interesting results, and to throw light on subjects apparently unconnected with them, no apology can be needed for inviting attention to any branch of that curious and interesting study, the anatomy, as it may be called, of the human mind.

REMARKS

ON SOME OF THE

CHARACTERS OF SHAKESPERE.

———◆———

INTRODUCTION.

THE writers upon dramatic composition have, for the most part, confined their observations to the fable; and the maxims received amongst them, for the conduct of it, are therefore emphatically called, *The Rules of the Drama*. It has been found easy to give and to apply them; they are obvious, they are certain, they are general: and poets without genius have, by observing them, pretended to fame; while critics without discernment have assumed importance from knowing them. But the regularity thereby established, though highly proper, is by no means the first requisite in a dramatic composition. Even waving all consideration of those finer feelings which a poet's imagination or sensibility imparts, there is, within the colder provinces of judgment and of knowledge, a subject for criticism, more worthy of attention than the common topics of discussion: I mean the distinction and preservation of *character*, without which the piece is at best a tale, not an action; for the actors in it are not produced upon the scene. They were distinguished by character; all men are; by that we know them, by that we are interested in their fortunes; by that their conduct, their sentiments, their very language is formed: and whenever therefore, the proper marks of it are missing, we immediately perceive that the person before our eyes is but supposititious. Experience has shown, that however rigidly, and however rightly, the unities of action, time, and place, have been insisted on, they may be dispensed with, and the magic of the scene may make the absurdity invisible. Most of Shakespere's Plays abound with instances of such a fascination. It is certain, too, that it is not always necessary strongly to affect, in order warmly to interest, the spectators; for many tragedies, which are not pathetic, are yet very engaging; and many comedies are amusing, though almost destitute of humour: and as to the beauties of poetry and of fancy, in some very fit subjects for a theatrical exhibition they cannot be properly admitted ; and very few absolutely require them. But variety and truth of character are indispensably necessary to all, both to comedy and to tragedy; and none of them deserve their name any further than this merit belongs to them. Incidents, images, passions, language, and numbers, are common to dramatic and to other compositions; they might all be introduced into the *relation* of an affecting story; but characters can never be perfectly exhibited, except in a drama. When they, therefore, are wanting, the want cannot be supplied, nor can it be concealed; the delusion fails, and the interest ceases; the performers can only recite, they have nothing to act: for the performance is but a dialogue, not a representation; and must be received by the disappointed spectators, at the best, with indifference.

By the feeble attempts which every dramatic writer makes to characterize his personages, and by the rude sketches which some critics have drawn of a few dramatic characters, the truth of these principles is acknowledged, but the extent of them is not illustrated: for general marks of distinction do not denote the individual, but only shew the class he belongs to. Men differ as much in their minds as in their faces; and to each man belong some general marks of distinction in both: his complexion is brown, or it is fair; his features are hard, or soft; and there is an expression of vivacity, of sensibility, or of vacancy, in the construction and motion of his eyes. But faces, agreeing in many such circumstances, are not therefore, upon the whole, like to each other: nor would a picture be the portrait of any individual, to whom, in all these, and in many more particulars, it were similar, unless the painter had also caught those peculiarities of countenance, which distinguish that person from all others who have the same cast of features, and the same tint of complexion. In like manner do the minds of men differ from each other. There are in these also general marks of distinction; quickness, or clearness, or want of apprehension; a severity or a mildness of temper; tenderness or violence in the passions. But no assemblage of these will together form the character of any individual: for he has some predominant principle; there is a certain proportion in which his qualities are mixed; and each affects the other. Those qualities check that principle, though at the same time they are themselves controlled by it: for nothing is absolutely pure and simple in its composition; and therefore if his peculiarities do not appear, no resemblance of him can be seen.

The force of character is so strong, that the most violent passions do not prevail over it; on the contrary, it directs them, and gives a particular turn to all their operations. The most pathetic expressions, therefore, of the passions are not true, if they are not accommodated to the character of the person supposed to feel them; and the effect upon the spectators will be weak, when so much of the reality is wanting in the imitation. Such general expressions of the passions, are, in poetry, like those which in painting are called *studies*, and which, unless they are adapted to the features, circumstances, and dispositions of the several personages, to whose figures they are applied, remain mere studies still, and do not connect with the portrait or history-piece into which they are introduced.

Yet the generality of dramatic writers, and more especially of those who have chosen tragedy for their subject, have contented themselves with the distant resemblance, which indiscriminate expressions of passion, and imperfect, because general, marks of character can give. Elevated ideas become the hero; a professed contempt of all principles denotes a villain; frequent gusts of rage betray a violence, and tender sentiments show a mildness, of disposition. But a villain differs not more from a saint, than he does in some particulars from another as ba as himself: and the same degrees of anger, excited by the same occasions, break forth in as many several shapes, as there are various tempers. But these distinguishing peculiarities between man and man have too often escaped the observation of tragic writers. The comic writers have, indeed, frequently caught them; but then they are apt to fall into an excess the other way, and overcharge their imitations: they do not suffer a character to show itself, but are continually pointing it out to observation; and by thus bidding the spectator take notice of the likeness, tell him all the while that it is but a representation. The former is commonly the defect of the French tragedies, which are therefore insipid, even when they abound with poetry and passion: and the latter is a fault common in the English comedies, which makes them disgusting, though they are full of wit, good sense, and humour. The one falls short of character, the other runs into caricature; that wants resemblance, and this is mere mimicry.

Shakespere has generally avoided both extremes; and, however faulty in some respects, is in this, the most essential part of the drama, considered as a representation, excellent beyond comparison. No other dramatic writer could ever pretend to so deep and so extensive a knowledge of the human heart; and he had a genius to express all that his penetration could discover. The characters therefore which he has drawn, are masterly copies from nature; differing each from the other, and animated as the originals, though correct to a scrupulous precision. The truth and force of the imitation recommend it as a subject worthy of criticism: and though it admits not of such general rules as the conduct of the fable, yet every several character furnishing a variety of remarks, the mind, by attending to them, acquires a turn to such observations; than which nothing is more agreeable or more useful in forming the judgment, whether on real characters in life, or dramatic representations of them. To give the mind this turn is the design of the following pages.

REMARKS, &c.

———◆———

Every Play of Shakespere abounds with instances of his excellence in distinguishing characters. It would be difficult to determine which is the most striking of all that he drew; but his merit will appear most conspicuously by comparing two opposite characters, who happen to be placed in similar circumstances:—not that on such occasions he marks them more strongly than on others, but because the contrast makes the distinction more apparent; and of these none seem to agree so much in situation, and to differ so much in disposition, as Richard the Third and Macbeth. Both are soldiers, both usurpers; both attain the throne by the same means, by treason and murder; and both lose it too in the same manner, in battle against the person claiming it as lawful heir. Perfidy, violence and tyranny are common to both; and those only, their obvious qualites, would have been attributed indiscriminately to both by an ordinary dramatic writer. But Shakespere, in conformity to the truth of history, as far as it led him, and by improving upon the fables which have been blended with it, has ascribed opposite principles and motives to the same designs and actions, and various effects to the operation of the same events upon different tempers. Richard and Macbeth, as represented by him, agree in nothing but their fortunes.

The periods of history, from which the subjects are taken, are such as at the best can be depended on only for some principal facts; but not for the minute detail, by which characters are unravelled. That of Macbeth is too distant to be particular; that of Richard, too full of discord and animosity to be true: and antiquity has not feigned more circumstances of horror in the one, than party violence has given credit to in the other. Fiction has even gone so far as to introduce supernatural fables into both stories: the usurpation of Macbeth is said to have been foretold by some witches; and the tyranny of Richard by omens attending his birth. From these fables, Shakespere, unrestrained and indeed uninformed by history, seems to have taken the hint of their several characters; and he has adapted their dispositions so as to give to such fictions, in the days he wrote, a show of probability. The first thought of acceding to the throne is suggested, and success in the attempt is promised, to Macbeth by the witches: he is therefore represented as a man, whose natural temper would have deterred him from such a design, if he had not been immediately tempted, and strongly impelled to it. Richard, on the other hand, brought with him into the world the signs of ambition and cruelty: his disposition, therefore, is suited to those symptoms; and he is not discouraged from indulging it by the improbability of succeeding, or by any difficulties and dangers which obstruct his way.

Agreeable to these ideas, Macbeth appears to be a man not destitute of the feelings of humanity. His lady gives him that character.

———I fear thy nature;
It is too full o' the milk of human kindness,
To catch the nearest way*.———

Which apprehension was well founded; for his reluctance to commit the murder is owing in a great measure to reflections which arise from sensibility:

---

* Macbeth, Act I. sc. 7.

> ——————He's here in double trust:
> First, as I am his kinsman and his subject;
> Strong both against the deed; then as his host,
> Who should against his murderer shut the door,
> Not bear the knife myself*.——

Immediately after he tells Lady Macbeth,—

> We will proceed no further in this business;
> He hath honoured me of late†.

And thus giving way to his natural feelings of kindred, hospitality, and gratitude, he for a while lays aside his purpose. A man of such a disposition will esteem, as they ought to be esteemed, all gentle and amiable qualities in another: and therefore Macbeth is affected by the mild virtues of Duncan; and reveres them in his sovereign when he stifles them in himself. That

> ——————This Duncan
> Hath borne his faculties so meekly; hath been
> So clear in his great office,‡—

---

* Macbeth, Act I. sc. 10.   † Ibid. Act I. sc. 9.
‡ Ibid. Act I. sc. 10.

is one of his reasons against the murder: and when he is tortured with the thought of Banquo's issue succeeding him in the throne, he aggravates his misery by observing, that,

For them the gracious Duncan have I murder'd;*

which epithet of *gracious* would not have occurred to one who was not struck with the particular merit it expresses.

The frequent references to the prophecy in favour of Banquo's issue, is another symptom of the same disposition: for it is not always from fear, but sometimes from envy, that he alludes to it: and being himself very susceptible of those domestic affections, which raise a desire and love of posterity, he repines at the succession assured to the family of his rival, and which in his estimation seems more valuable

---

* Macbeth, Act III. sc. 2.

than his own actual possession. He therefore reproaches the sisters for their partiality, when

> Upon my head they plac'd a fruitless crown,
> And put a barren sceptre in my gripe,
> Thence to be wrench'd with an unlineal hand,
> No son of mine succeeding. If 'tis so,
> For Banquo's issue have I 'fil'd my mind,
> For them the gracious Duncan have I murder'd;
> Put rancours in the vessel of my peace
> Only for them; and mine eternal jewel
> Given to the common enemy of man,
> To make them kings, the seed of Banquo kings!
> Rather than so, come, Fate, into the list,
> And champion me to the utterance.*——

Thus, in a variety of instances, does the tenderness in his character shew itself; and one who has these feelings, though he may have no principles, cannot easily be induced to commit a murder. The intervention of a supernatural cause accounts for his acting so contrary to his disposition. But that alone is not sufficient to

---

* Macbeth, Act III. sc. 2.

prevail entirely over his nature: the instigations of his wife are also necessary to keep him to his purpose; and she, knowing his temper, not only stimulates his courage to the deed, but, sensible that, besides a backwardness in daring, he had a degree of softness which wanted hardening, endeavours to remove all remains of humanity from his breast, by the horrid comparison she makes between him and herself:

> ————I have given suck, and know
> How tender 'tis to love the babe that milks me:
> I would, while it was smiling in my face,
> Have pluck'd my nipple from his boneless gums,
> And dash'd the brains out, had I but so sworn
> As you have done to this.*————

The argument is, that the strongest and most natural affections are to be stifled upon so great an occasion: and such an argument is proper to persuade one who is liable to be swayed

---

* Macbeth, Act I. sc. 10.

by them; but is no incentive either to his courage or his ambition.

Richard is in all these particulars the very reverse to Macbeth. He is totally destitute of every softer feeling:

> I that have neither pity, love, nor fear,*

is the character he gives of himself, and which he preserves throughout; insensible to his habitudes with a brother, to his connexion with a wife, to the piety of the king, and the innocence of the babes, whom he murders. The deformity of his body was supposed to indicate a similar depravity of mind; and Shakespere makes great use both of that, and of the current stories of the times concerning the circumstances of his birth, to intimate that his actions proceeded not from the occasion, but from a

---

* 3 Henry VI. Act V. sc. 7.

savageness of nature. Henry therefore tells him,

> Thy mother felt more than a mother's pain,
> And yet brought forth less than a mother's hope;
> To wit, an indigested, deform'd lump,
> Not like the fruit of such a goodly tree.
> Teeth hadst thou in thy head when thou wast born,
> To signify thou cam'st to bite the world;
> And, if the rest be true which I have heard,
> Thou cam'st into the world with thy legs forward.*

Which violent invective does not affect Richard as a reproach; it serves him only for a pretence to commit the murder he came resolved on and his answer while he is killing Henry is,

> I'll hear no more; die, prophet, in thy speech!
> For this, among the rest, was I ordain'd.†

Immediately afterwards he resumes the subject himself; and, priding himself that the signs

---

* 3 Henry VI. Act V. sc. 7.　　　† Ibid.

given at his birth were verified in his conduct, he says,

> Indeed 'tis true that Henry told me of;
> For I have often heard my mother say,
> I came into the world with my legs forward.
> Had I not reason, think ye, to make haste,
> And seek their ruin that usurp'd our right?
> The midwife wonder'd; and the women cried,
> O Jesus bless us! he is born with teeth!
> And so I was; which plainly signified
> That I should snarl, and bite, and play the dog.
> Then, since the heavens have shap'd my body so,
> Let hell make crook'd my mind to answer it.[*]

Several other passages to the same effect imply that he has a natural propensity to evil; crimes are his delight: but Macbeth is always in an agony when he thinks of them. He is sensible, before he proceeds, of

> ———the heat-oppressed brain.[†]

---

[*] 3 Henry VI. Act V. sc. 7.   [†] Macbeth, Act II. sc. 2.

He feels

>———The present horror of the time
Which now suits with it.*———

And immediately after he has committed the murder, he is

>———afraid to think what he has done.†

He is pensive even while he is enjoying the effect of his crimes; but Richard is in spirits merely at the prospect of committing them; and what is effort in the one, is sport to the other. An extraordinary gaiety of heart shews itself upon those occasions, which to Macbeth seem most awful; and whether he forms or executes, contemplates the means, or looks back on the success, of the most wicked and desperate designs, they are at all times to him subjects of merriment. Upon parting from his brother, he bids him

---

* Macbeth, Act II. sc. 2. † Ibid. sc. 3.

> Go, tread the path that thou shalt ne'er return;
> Simple, plain Clarence! I do love thee so,
> That I will shortly send thy soul to heaven,
> If heaven will take the present at our hands.*

His amusement, when he is meditating the murder of his nephews, is the application of some proverbs to their discourse and situation:

> So wise, so young, they say, do ne'er live long.†

And,

> Short summer lightly has a forward spring.‡

His ironical address to Tyrrel,

> Dar'st thou resolve to kill a friend of mine?||

is agreeable to the rest of his deportment: and his pleasantry does not forsake him when he considers some of his worst deeds, after he has

---

* Richard III. Act I. sc. 1. † Ibid. Act III. sc. 1. ‡ Ibid.
|| Ibid. Act IV. sc. 2.

committed them; for the terms in which he mentions them are, that,

> The sons of Edward sleep in Abraham's bosom;
> And Ann my wife hath bid the world good night.*

But he gives a still greater loose to his humour, when his deformity, and the omens attending his birth, are alluded to, either by himself or by others, as symptoms of the wickedness of his nature. The ludicrous turn which he gives to the reproach of Henry has been quoted already; and his joy at gaining the consent of Lady Ann to marry him, together with his determination to get rid of her, are expressed in the same wanton vein, when amongst other sallies of exultation, he says,

> Was ever woman in this humour woo'd?
> Was ever woman in this humour won?
> I'll have her, but I will not keep her long:
> What! I that kill'd her husband and her father,
> To take her in her heart's extremest hate,
> With curses in her mouth, tears in her eyes,

---

* Richard III. Act IV. sc. 3.

> The bleeding witness of her hatred by!
> With God, her conscience, and these bars against me,
> And I no friends to back my suit withal,
> But the plain Devil, and dissembling looks,
> And yet to win her,—All the world to nothing!—
> My dukedom to a beggarly denier,
> I do mistake my person all this while!
> Upon my life, she finds, although I cannot,
> Myself to be a marvellous proper man!
> I'll be at charges for a looking-glass,
> And entertain a score or two of taylors
> To study fashions to adorn my body.*

And yet, that nothing might be wanting to make him completely odious, Shakespere has very artfully mixed with all this ridicule, a rancorous envy of those who have greater advantages of figure.

> To shrink mine arm up like a wither'd shrub;
> To make an envious mountain on my back,
> Where sits deformity to mock my body! †

and,

> I, that am curtail'd of this fair proportion,
> Cheated of feature by dissembling nature,

---

* Richard III. Act I. sc. 2.　　† 3 Henry VI. Act III. sc. 3.

> Deform'd, unfinish'd, sent before my time
> Into this breathing world, scarce half made up,
> And that so lamely and unfashionably,
> That dogs bark at me, as I halt by them,[*]

are starts of spleen which he determines to vent on such

> As are of better person than himself.[†]

There is, besides, another subject on which he sometimes exercises his wit, which is his own hypocrisy. I shall have occasion hereafter to take more notice of that part of his character; at present it is sufficient to observe, that to himself he laughs at the sanctified appearances which he assumes, and makes ridiculous applications of that very language by which he imposed upon others. His answer to his mother's blessing,

---

[*] Richard III. Act I. sc. 1.   [†] 3 Henry VI. Act III. sc. 3.

> Amen! and make me die a good old man!
> This is the butt-end of a mother's blessing;
> I marvel that her grace should leave it out,*

is an example both of his hypocrisy and his humour: his application of the story of Judas to the affection he had just before expressed for Edward's family,

> To say the truth, so Judas kiss'd his master;
> And cried, All hail! when as he meant all harm, †

is another instance of the same kind; and there are many more. But still all this turn to ridicule does not proceed from levity; for Macbeth, though always serious, is not so considerate and attentive in times of action and business. But Richard, when he is indulging that wickedness and malice, which he is so prone to and fond of, expresses his enjoyment of it by such sallies of

---

* Richard III. Act II. sc. 3. † 3 Henry VI. Act V. sc. 8.

humour; on other occasions he is alert, on these only is he gay; and the delight he takes in them gives an air to his whole demeanour, which induces Hastings to observe, that as

> His Grace looks cheerfully and well this morning :
> There's some conceit or other likes him well,
> When that he bids good-morrow with such spirit; *

which observation is made at the moment when he was meditating, and but just before he accomplished, the destruction of the nobleman who makes it. That Macbeth, on the other hand, is constantly shocked and depressed with those circumstances which inspire Richard with extravagant mirth and spirits, is so obvious, that more quotations are unnecessary to prove it.

The total insensibility to every tender feeling, which distinguishes the character of Richard, makes him consider the mild virtues of Henry

---

* Richard III. Act III. sc. 3.

as so many weaknesses, and insult him for them, at the very moment when they would have been allowed all their merit, and have attracted some compassion from any other person.

> See how my sword weeps for the poor king's death!*

is the taunt he utters over his bloody corse: and when afterwards Lady Ann aggravates the assassination of Henry, by exclaiming,

> O he was gentle, mild, and virtuous!†

his answer is, that he was therefore

> The fitter for the King of Heaven that hath him!‡

Richard despises Henry for his meekness, and turns it into a jest, when it is urged against himself as a matter of reproach. But Macbeth

---

* 3 Henry VI. Act V. sc. 7.   † Richard III. Act I. sc. 2.
‡ Richard III. Act I. sc. 2.

esteems Duncan for the same quality; and of himself, without being reminded, reflects upon it with contrition.

It would have been an inconsistency to have attributed to Richard any of those domestic affections which are proper in Macbeth: nor are they only omitted; but Shakespere has with great nicety shown, that his zeal for his family springs not from them, but from his ambition, and from that party-spirit which the contention between the Houses of York and Lancaster had inspired. His animosity therefore is inveterate against all

―― who wish the downfall of our House;*

and he eagerly pursues their destruction, as the means of his own advancement. But his desire for the prosperity of his family goes no further:

---

* 3 Henry VI. Act V. sc. 7.

the execration he utters against his brother Edward,

> Would he were wasted, marrow, bones, and all! *

is to the full as bitter as any against the Lancastrians. The fear of children from Edward's marriage provokes him to this curse; yet not a wish for posterity from his own marriage ever crosses him: and though childless himself, he does not hesitate to destroy the heirs of his family. He would annihilate the House he had fought for all his life, rather than be disappointed of the throne he aspired to; and after he had ascended it, he forgets the interests of that House, whose accession had opened the way to his usurpation. He does not provide, he does not wish, for its continuance; the possession, not the descent, of the crown is his object: and when afterwards it is disputed with him, he considers Richmond only

---

* 3 Henry VI. Act III. sc. 3.

as a pretender. The circumstance of his being also a Lancaster does not occur to him; and he even, when he seems to contemn him more, does not hate him so much as he did Henry, though Richmond was far the less amiable, as well as the less despicable, of the two: all which conduct tallies with the principle he avows, when he declares,

> I have no brother, I am like no brother:
> And this word love, which grey-beards call divine,
> Be resident in men like one another,
> And not in me : I am myself alone.*

But the characters of Richard and Macbeth are marked not only by opposite qualities; but even the same qualities in each differ so much in the cause, the kind, and the degree, that the distinction in them is as evident as in the others. Ambition is common to both; but in

---

* 3 Henry VI. Act V. sc. 7.

Macbeth it proceeds only from vanity, which is flattered and satisfied by the splendour of a throne: in Richard it is founded upon pride: his ruling passion is the lust of power:

> ———this earth affords no joy to him,
> But to command, to check, and to o'erbear.*

And so great is that joy, that he enumerates among the delights of war,

> To fright the souls of fearful adversaries;†

which is a pleasure brave men do not very sensibly feel; they rather value

> ——— Battles
> Nobly, hardly fought.———

But, in Richard, the sentiments natural to his high courage are lost in the greater satisfaction of trampling on mankind, and seeing even those whom he despises crouching beneath him; at

---

* 3 Henry VI. Act. III. sc. 3.   † Richard III. Act I. sc. 1.

the same time, to submit himself to any authority, is incompatible with his eager desire of ruling over all; nothing less than the first place can satiate his love of dominion: he declares that he shall

> Count himself but bad, till he is best:*

and,

> While I live account this world but hell,
> Until the misshap'd trunk that bears this head
> Be round impaled with a glorious crown.†

Which crown he hardly ever mentions, except in swelling terms of exultation; and which, even after he has obtained it, he calls

> The high imperial type of this earth's glory.‡

But the crown is not Macbeth's pursuit through life: he had never thought of it till it

---

* 3 Henry VI. Act V. sc. 7.   † Ibid.
‡ Richard III. Act IV. sc. 5.

was suggested to him by the witches; he receives their promise, and the subsequent earnest of the truth of it, with calmness. But his wife, whose thoughts are always more aspiring, hears the tidings with rapture, and greets him with the most extravagant congratulations; she complains of his moderation; the utmost merit she can allow him is, that he is

———— not without ambition.*

But it is cold and faint, for the subject of it is that of a weak mind; it is only preeminence of place, not dominion. He never carries his idea beyond the honour of the situation he aims at; and therefore he considers it as a situation which Lady Macbeth will partake of equally with him: and in his letter tells her,

---

* Macbeth, Act I. sc. 7.

> This have I thought good to deliver thee, my dearest partner of greatness, that thou mightest not lose the dues of rejoicing, by being ignorant of what greatness is promised thee.*

But it was his rank alone, not his power, in which she could share: and that indeed is all which he afterwards seems to think he had attained by his usurpation. He styles himself,

> —— high-plac'd Macbeth:†

but in no other light does he ever contemplate his advancement with satisfaction; and when he finds that it is not attended with that adulation and respect which he had promised himself, and which would have soothed his vanity, he sinks under the disappointment, and complains that

---

* Macbeth, Act I. sc. 7.   † Ibid. Act IV. sc. 2.

> ——— my way of life
> Is fallen into the sear, the yellow leaf;
> And that which should accompany old age,
> As honour, love, obedience, troops of friends,
> I must not look to have.*———

These blessings, so desirable to him, are widely different from the pursuits of Richard. He wishes not to gain the affections, but to secure the submission of his subjects, and is happy to see men shrink under his control. But Macbeth, on the contrary, reckons among the miseries of his condition

> ——— —— mouth-honour, breath,
> Which the poor heart would fain deny, but dare not:†

and pities the wretch who fears him.

The towering ambition of Richard, and the weakness of that passion in Macbeth, are further

---

* Macbeth, Act V. sc. 3. † Ibid.

instances wherein Shakespere has accommodated their characters to the fabulous parts of their stories. The necessity for the most extraordinary incitements to stimulate the latter, thereby becomes apparent; and the meaning of the omens, which attended the birth of the former, is explained. Upon the same principle, a distinction still stronger is made in the article of courage, though both are possessed of it even to an eminent degree; but in Richard it is intrepidity, and in Macbeth no more than resolution: in him it proceeds from exertion, not from nature; in enterprise he betrays a degree of fear, though he is able, when occasion requires, to stifle and subdue it. When he and his wife are concerting the murder, his doubt,

——————— If we should fail,*

---

* Macbeth, Act I. sc. 10.

is a difficulty raised by apprehension; and as soon as that is removed by the contrivance of Lady Macbeth, to make the officers drunk, and lay the crime upon them, he runs with violence into the other extreme of confidence, and cries out, with a rapture unusual to him,

> ——Bring forth men-children only!
> For thy undaunted metal should compose
> Nothing but males. Will it not be receiv'd,
> When we have mark'd with blood these sleepy two
> Of his own chamber, and us'd their very daggers,
> That they have done it?*——

Which question he puts to her, who but the moment before had suggested the thought of

> His spongy officers, who shall bear the guilt
> Of our great quell.†——

And his asking it again proceeds from that extravagance, with which a delivery from appre-

---

* Macbeth, Act I. sc. 10. † Ibid.

hension and doubt is always accompanied. Then summoning all his fortitude, he says,

> ——I am settled, and bend up
> Each corporal agent to this terrible feat;*

and proceeds to the bloody business without any further recoils. But a certain degree of restlessness and anxiety still continues, such as is constantly felt by a man not naturally very bold, worked up to a momentous achievement. His imagination dwells entirely on the circumstances of horror which surround him; the vision of the dagger; the darkness and the stillness of the night; and the terrors and the prayers of the chamberlains. Lady Macbeth, who is cool and undismayed, attends to the business only; considers of the place where she had laid the daggers ready; the impossibility of his missing them; and is afraid of nothing

---

* Macbeth, Act I. sc. 10.

but a disappointment. She is earnest and eager; he is uneasy and impatient, and therefore wishes it over:

> I go, and it is done; the bell invites me.
> Hear it not, Duncan, for it is a knell
> Which summons thee to heaven or to hell.*

But a resolution, thus forced, cannot hold longer than the immediate occasion for it: the moment after that is accomplished for which it was necessary, his thoughts take the contrary turn, and he cries out in agony and despair,

> Wake, Duncan, with this knocking; would thou could'st!†

That courage, which had supported him while he was *settled and bent up*, forsakes him so immediately after he has performed the *terrible feat* for which it had been exerted, that he forgets the favourite circumstance of laying it

---

* Macbeth, Act II. sc. 2. † Ibid. sc. 3.

on the officers of the bed-chamber; and when reminded of it, he refuses to return and complete his work, acknowledging that

> I am afraid to think what I have done;
> Look on't again I dare not.*——

His disordered senses deceive him, and his debilitated spirits fail him; he owns that

> ——every noise appals him.†

He listens when nothing stirs; he mistakes the sounds he does hear; he is so confused, as not to distinguish whence the knocking proceeds. She, who is more calm, knows that it is at the south entry; she gives clear and direct answers to all the incoherent questions he asks her: but he returns none to that which she puts to him; and though after some time, and when necessity again urges him to recollect himself, he recovers so far as to conceal his distress, yet he still is

---

* Macbeth, Act II. sc. 3.   † Ibid.

not able to divert his thoughts from it: all his answers to the trivial questions of Lenox and Macduff are evidently given by a man thinking of something else; and by taking a tincture from the subject of his attention, they become equivocal:

Macd. Is the king stirring, worthy Thane?
Macb. Not yet.
Len. Goes the king hence to-day?
Macb. He did appoint so.
Len. The night has been unruly; where we lay,
Our chimneys were blown down; and, as they say,
Lamentings heard i' the air, strange screams of death,
And prophesying, with accents terrible,
Of dire combustions, and confus'd events,
New hatch'd to th' woful time. The obscure bird
Clamour'd the live-long night. Some say the earth
Was fev'rous, and did shake.
Macb. 'Twas a rough night.
Len. My young remembrance cannot parallel
A fellow to it.[*]

---

[*] Macbeth, Act II. sc. 4.

Not yet, implies that he will by and by, and is a kind of guard against any suspicion of his knowing that the king would never stir more: *He did appoint so,* is the very counterpart of that which he had said to Lady Macbeth, when, on his first meeting her, she asked him,

> *Lady.* When goes he hence?
> *Macb.* To-morrow, as he purposes.*

In both which answers he alludes to his disappointing the king's intention. And when forced to make some reply to the long description given by Lenox, he puts off the subject which the other was so much inclined to dwell upon, by a slight acquiescence in what had been said of the roughness of the night; but not like a man who had been attentive to the account, or was willing to keep up the conversation.

---

* Macbeth, Act I. sc. 7.

Nothing can be conceived more directly opposite to the agitations of Macbeth's mind, than the serenity of Richard in parallel circumstances. Upon the murder of the Prince of Wales, he immediately resolves on the assassination of Henry; and stays only to say to Clarence,

Rich. Clarence, excuse me to the king my brother;
I'll hence to London on a serious matter:
Ere ye come there, be sure to hear some news.
   Cla. What? What?
   Rich. The Tower, man, the Tower! I'll root them out.*

It is a thought of his own, which just then occurs to him: he determines upon it without hesitation: it requires no consideration, and admits of no delay: he is eager to put it in execution; but his eagerness proceeds from ardour, not from anxiety; and is not hurry, but

---

* 3 Henry VI. Act V. sc. 6.

dispatch. He does not wait to communicate to the king his brother; he only hints the thought as he had conceived it, to Clarence; and supposes that the name alone of the Tower will sufficiently indicate his business there. When come thither, he proceeds directly without relenting; it is not to him, as to Macbeth, *a terrible feat*, but only a *serious matter;* and,

> Sir, leave us to ourselves, we must confer,

is all the preparation he makes for it; and indeed with him it is little more than a conference with an enemy: his animosity and his insolence are the same, both before and after the assassination; and nothing retards, staggers, or alarms him. The humour which breaks from him, upon this and other occasions, has been taken notice of already, as a mark of his depravity; it is at the same time a proof of his calmness, and of the composure he preserves when he does not indulge himself in ridicule. It is with the most unfeeling steadiness that he tells the first tidings of the death of Clarence to Edward, when, on the Queen's intercession in his favour, he occasionally introduces it as a notorious fact, and tells her,

> Who knows not that the gentle duke is dead?
> You do him injury to scorn his corse. *

He feels no remorse for the deed, nor fear of discovery; and therefore does not drop a word which can betray him, but artfully endeavours to impute it to others; and, without the least appearance of ostentation, makes the most natural and most pertinent reflections upon the fruits of rashness, and the vengeance of God against such offenders. The same determined spirit carries him through the bloody business of murdering his nephews; and when Buck-

---

* Richard III. Act II. sc. 1.

ingham shows a reluctance to be concerned in it, he immediately looks out for another: some

>   ——————iron-witted fool,
>   Or unrespective boy,*

more apt for his purpose. Had Macbeth been thus disappointed in the person to whom he had opened himself, it would have disconcerted any design he had formed: but Richard does not suffer such an accident to delay his pursuit for a moment; he only wonders at the folly of the man, and says,

> Hath he so long held out with me untir'd,
> And stops he now for breath? Well, be it so.†

And having found a person ready to undertake the business, he declines the participation of Buckingham, who comes back disposed to comply with his request; and though the deed

---

* Richard III. Act IV. sc. 2. † Ibid.

is still undone, and Buckingham is apprised of his intention to do it, he is not deterred by the fear of being prevented in this, or exposed for his other crimes, from mortally offending his powerful accomplice by a breach of the promise he had made him; and aggravates the offence he gives, by the manner of it; first treating him with contempt, and then in anger telling him,

> Thou troublest me; I am not in the vein.*

When afterwards Tyrrel returns to inform him that he has executed his commission, so far is he from being *afraid to think what he has done*, that he is curious to inquire into the particulars of the proceeding; and though certain of the event, is solicitous to hear at leisure in what manner it was conducted:

---

* Richard III. Act IV. sc. 2.

Rich. Kind Tyrrel! am I happy in thy news?

Tyr. If to have done the thing you gave in charge
Beget your happiness, be happy then,
For it is done.——

Rich. But didst thou see them dead?

Tyr. I did, my lord.

Rich. And buried, gentle Tyrrel?

Tyr. The chaplain of the Tower hath buried them;
But where, to say the truth, I do not know.

Rich. Come to me, Tyrrel, soon; soon after supper,
When thou shalt tell the process of their death.[*]

It is needless to refer to other instances of the same resolute behaviour. He never deviates; but throughout the whole progress of his reiterated crimes, he is not once daunted at the danger, discouraged by the difficulties, nor disconcerted by the accidents attending them; nor ever shocked either at the idea or the reflection.

Macbeth indeed commits subsequent murders with less agitation than that of Duncan: but this

---

[*] Richard III. Act IV. sc. 3.

is no inconsistency in his character; on the contrary, it confirms the principles upon which it is formed; for besides his being hardened to the deeds of death, he is impelled to the perpetration of them by other motives than those which instigated him to assassinate his sovereign. In the one he sought to gratify his ambition; the rest are for his security: and he gets rid of fear by guilt, which, to a mind so constituted, may be the less uneasy sensation of the two. The anxiety which prompts him to the destruction of Banquo, arises entirely from apprehension:

>   ————to be thus, is nothing;
> But to be safely thus:—our fears in Banquo
> Stick deep; and in his royalty of nature
> Reigns that which would be fear'd. 'Tis much he dares;
> And to that dauntless temper of his mind,
> He hath a wisdom that doth guide his valour
> To act in safety. There is none but he
> Whose being I do fear; and under him
> My genius is rebuk'd.*——

---

* Macbeth, Act III. sc. 2.

For though one principal reason of his jealousy was the impression made on Macbeth's mind, by the prophecy of the witches in favour of Banquo's issue; yet here starts forth another, quite consistent with a temper not quite free from timidity. He is afraid of him personally: that fear is founded on the superior courage of the other, and he feels himself under an awe before him; a situation which a dauntless spirit can never get into. So great are these terrors, that he betrays them to the murderers, by telling them,

> We wear our health but sickly in his life,
> Which in his death were perfect.*

And,

> ——every minute of his being thrusts
> Against my near'st of life.†——

---

* Macbeth, Act III. sc. 2.   † Ibid.

To Lady Macbeth he confesses that

>———full of scorpions is his mind:*

and declares, that he will never

> ———eat his meal in fear, and sleep
> In the affliction of these terrible dreams
> That shake him nightly.†———

But as the murder is for his own security, the same apprehensions which checked him in his designs upon Duncan, impel him to this upon Banquo. He has no occasion for the instigations of his wife; he can even withhold the secret from her, that he may greet her with the welcome news after the deed is done; and only intimates that,

> ———ere to black Hecate's summons
> The shard-born beetle with his drowsy hums
> Hath rung night's yawning peal, there shall be done
> A deed of dreadful note.

---

* Macbeth, Act. III. sc. 3.   † Ibid.

> *Lady.* What's to be done?
> *Macb.* Be innocent of the knowledge, dearest chuck,
> Till thou applaud the deed.*——

And when the murderer comes to tell him that the father is killed, but that the son escaped; though he perceives the prophecy still keeps its force, and laments his situation, yet he immediately recovers, on the reflection of his delivery from the apprehension of Banquo personally; and asks again,

> ————But Banquo's safe?
> *Murd.* Aye, my good lord, safe in a ditch he lies,
> With twenty trenched gashes in his head,
> The least a death to nature.
> *Macb.* Thanks for that;
> There the grown serpent lies: the worm that's fled
> Hath nature that in time will venom breed,
> No teeth for the present.†——

Throughout the whole transaction, his principal object is the death of the father; and the

---

* Macbeth, Act III. sc. 5. † Ibid.

securing of his crown against Banquo's issue, who alone were pointed out to his jealousy by the witches, is no more than a secondary consideration.

The same motives of personal fear, and those unmixed with any other, impel him to seek the destruction of Macduff: his answer to the apparition, who warns him to beware of the Thane of Fife, is,

> Whate'er thou art, for thy good caution, thanks;
> Thou'st harp'd my fear aright.*

And when, soon afterwards, he is told by another apparition, that "none of woman born should harm Macbeth," though he then believed, and through his whole life confided, in that assurance, yet his anxiety to be out of the reach of danger immediately recurs again, and makes him revert to his former resolution.

---

* Macbeth, Act IV. sc. 2.

His reflections upon receiving the promise prove both his credulity and his timidity; for he says,

> Then live, Macduff; what need I fear of thee?
> And yet I'll make assurance doubly sure,
> And take a bond of fate: thou shalt not live;
> That I may tell pale-hearted fear, it lies,
> And sleep in spite of thunder.*——

That apprehension was his reason for these murders, he intimates himself; when meditating on that of Banquo, he observes, that

> Things bad begun, make strong themselves by ill.†

And when that of Macduff is in contemplation, he says,

> ———— I am in blood
> Stept in so far, that, should I wade no more,
> Returning were as tedious as going o'er.‡

In both instances he sacrifices the persons he fears to his safety.

---

* Macbeth, Act IV. sc. 2. † Ibid. Act III. sc. 3. ‡ Ibid. sc. 5.

But all the crimes Richard commits are for his advancement, not for his security: he is not drawn from one into another; but he premeditates several before he begins, and yet can look upon the distant prospect of a long succession of murders with steadiness and composure. Long before any decisive battle between the two Houses, he considers,

> ——between my soul's desire and me,
> Is Clarence, Henry, and his son young Edward,
> And all th' unlook'd-for issue of their bodies,
> To take their rooms, ere I can place myself.*

All these he kills, as occasions offer; he cuts off many others who arise to obstruct his deep-laid designs; and when at last, after he has attained the dignity to which he aspired, he determines to cut off his nephews, his motive is not self-preservation, but merely his establishment;

---

* 3 Henry VI. Act III. sc. 3.

and he breaks his purpose to Buckingham, by saying,

> Give me thy hand. Thus high, by thy advice,
> And thy assistance, is King Richard seated:
> But shall we wear these glories for a day?
> Or shall they last, and we rejoice in them?*

The danger of losing the great object of his ambition is that which alone alarms Richard: but Macbeth dreads the danger which threatens his life; and that terror constantly damps all the joys of his crown. When he says,

> ——Duncan is in his grave;
> After life's fretful fever, he sleeps well;
> Treason has done his worst; nor steel, nor poison,
> Malice domestic, foreign levy, nothing
> Can touch him further!†——

he only enumerates the mischiefs he fears; none of which are ever Richard's concern; those which are present he opposes with spirit, and

---

* Richard III. Act IV. sc. 2.   † Macbeth, Act III. sc. 3.

such as are imaginary never occur to him. He never provides against them; and while Macbeth's suspicions, the consequence of his apprehensions, extend to all his great lords, so that

> There's not a Thane of them, but in his house
> He keeps a servant fee'd;*——

Richard's dauntless nature sets him above all groundless surmises: and even when he receives information that he is betrayed, by the paper stuck upon the Duke of Norfolk's tent, to warn him not to expose himself too much in the cause of a master who is sold, he treats it slightly, as

> A thing devised by the enemy,†

and never thinks of it more.‡

---

* Macbeth, Act III. sc. 5.   † Richard III. Act V. sc. 6.

‡ His going round the camp, just before the battle, to listen if any meant to shrink from him, is proper on that particular occasion; it seems to be done without any premeditated design, and is very different from the constant jealousy of Macbeth.

Upon no occasion, however tremendous, and at no moment of his life, however unguarded, does he betray the least symptom of fear; whereas Macbeth is always shaken upon great, and frequently alarmed upon trivial, occasions. Upon the first meeting with the witches, he is agitated much more than Banquo; the one expresses mere curiosity, the other, astonishment: Banquo speaks to them first; and, the moment he sees them, asks them several particular and pertinent questions:

> ———What are these,
> So wither'd and so wild in their attire,
> That look not like inhabitants of earth,
> And yet are on't? Live you, or are you aught
> That man may question? You seem to understand me,
> By each at once her choppy finger laying
> Upon her skinny lips. You should be women,
> And yet your beards forbid me to interpret
> That you are so.*———

But Macbeth, though he has had time to recol-

---

* Macbeth, Act I. sc. 4.

lect himself, only repeats the same inquiry shortly; and bids them,

> Speak, if you can :—What are you? *

Which parts may appear to be injudiciously distributed; Macbeth being the principal personage in the play, and most immediately concerned in this particular scene; and it being to him that the witches first address themselves. But the difference in their characters accounts for such a distribution; Banquo being perfectly calm, and Macbeth a little ruffled by the adventure.† The distinction is preserved through the rest of their

---

* Macbeth, Act I. sc. 4.'

† Another instance of an effect produced by a distribution of the parts is in Act II. sc. 5, where, on Lady Macbeth's seeming to faint while Banquo and Macduff are solicitous about her, Macbeth, by his unconcern, betrays a consciousness that the fainting is feigned.

behaviour; for Banquo treats them with contempt, tells them that he

> ——neither begs, nor fears,
> Their favours, nor their hate; *——

which defiance seemed so bold to Macbeth, that he long after mentions it as an instance of his dauntless spirit, when he recollects that he

> ——chid the sisters.†

He considers them only as bubbles of the earth, such

> —— as the water has; ‡

ridicules their prophecy, by answering to Macbeth's question,

> —— Went it not so?
> *Banq.* To the self-same tune and words; §

---

* Macbeth, Act I. sc. 4.   † Ibid. Act III. sc. 2.
‡ Ibid. Act I. sc. 4.   § Ibid.

and still shows a disregard to it, even when it is in part fulfilled, by saying,

> What, can the devil speak true? *

But Macbeth is all the time far from possessing himself with such indifference; he is amazed when he perceives that they are vanished

> Into the air; and what seem'd corporal
> Melted, as breath into the wind; †

and is apparently troubled not only by their promise, but at their appearance. Upon the rising of Banquo's ghost, though that was a spectre which might well terrify him, yet he betrays a consciousness of too much natural timidity, by his peevish reproaches to Lady Macbeth, because she had not been so frightened as himself, when he tells her,

> —— you make me strange
> E'en to the disposition that I owe,

---

* Macbeth, Act I. sc. 5. † Ibid. sc. 4.

> When now I think you can behold such sights,
> And keep the natural ruby of your cheek,
> When mine is blanch'd with fear.*──

Another symptom of the same disposition is his catching the terrors he sees expressed in the countenance of the messenger, who informs him of the numbers of the enemy; and whom, in the most opprobrious language, he reviles for that

> ── those linen cheeks of thine
> Are counsellors to fear : †──

and immediately, on seeing this affrighted wretch, he himself sinks from the most assured confidence into the lowest despondency. These are all symptoms of timidity, which he confesses to have been natural to him, when he owns that

> The time has been, my senses would have cool'd
> To hear a night-shriek, and my fell of hair

---

* Macbeth, Act III. sc. 5.   † Ibid. Act V. sc. 3.

> Would at a dismal treatise rouse and stir,
> As life were in it.*──

But still he is able to suppress this natural timidity; he has an acquired, though not a constitutional, courage, which is equal to all ordinary occasions; and if it fails him upon those which are extraordinary, it is however so well formed, as to be easily resumed as soon as the shock is over. But his idea never rises above manliness of character, and he continually asserts his right to that character; which he would not do, if he did not take to himself a merit in supporting it.

> I dare do all that may become a man;
> Who dares do more, is none,†──

is his answer to the reproaches of Lady Macbeth, for want of spirit in the execution of his design upon Duncan. Upon the first appearance of

---

* Macbeth, Act V. sc. 5.   † Ibid. Act I. sc. 5.

Banquo's ghost, she endeavours to recover him from his terror, by summoning this consideration to his view:

> *Lady.* Are you a man?
> *Macb.* Aye, and a bold one, that dare look on that
> Which might appal the devil.*——

He puts in the same claim again, upon the ghost's rising again, and says,

> What man dare, I dare :——
> Take any shape but that, and my firm nerves
> Shall never tremble; be alive again,
> And dare me to the desert with thy sword:
> If trembling I inhibit, then protest me
> The baby of a girl : †——

and on its disappearing finally, he says,

> I am a man again.‡——

And even at the last, when he finds that the

---

* Macbeth, Act III. sc. 5. † Ibid. ‡ Ibid.

prophecy in which he had confided has deceived him by its equivocation, he bursts out into,

> Accursed be that tongue which tells me so,
> For it hath cow'd my better part of man!*

In all which passages he is apparently shaken out of that character to which he had formed himself; but for which he relied only on exertion of courage, without supposing insensibility to fear.

But Richard never stands in need of any affectation to others, or exertion in himself. Equal to every occasion, coolly contemplating the approaches of distant dangers, and unmoved amidst the most pressing—

> Promptus metuenda pati, si cominus instant;
> Aut deferre potest—— LUCAN.

he never thinks of behaving like a man, or is proud of doing so, for he cannot behave otherwise;

---

* Macbeth, Act V. sc. 7.

he contemns the most formidable enemies; by his account, it is only the *rash* or the *dull-brained* Buckingham, or the *shallow* Richmond, whom he has to contend with. He can despise for incapacity even the rightful heir to the crown he has usurped; and says of the son of Clarence,

> The boy is foolish, and I fear not him.*

He defies those who have most power to hurt him, as has been before observed of his behaviour to the Duke of Buckingham; and again appears in his frank reproaches to Lord Stanley, before he had taken a pledge for his fidelity: and when at last, by the appearance of all their ghosts whom he had murdered, he feels himself alarmed, he is yet so conscious of his general intrepidity, that he does not desire to conceal his agitation; and only wondering that he could fear, he tells Ratcliff,

> By the Apostle Paul, shadows to-night
> Have struck more terror to the soul of Richard,

---

* Richard III. Act IV. sc. 2.

Than can the substance of ten thousand soldiers,
Armed in proof, and led by shallow Richmond.*

But though Richard has no timidity in his nature which he wishes to conceal, yet he is conscious of other qualities, which it is necessary he should disguise; for if the wickedness of his heart had been fully known, he could not have hoped for success in his views: and he, therefore, from the beginning, covers his malice under an appearance of sanctity, which he himself thus describes:

— I sigh, and with a piece of Scripture
Tell them, that God bids us do good for evil:
And thus I clothe my naked villany
With old odd ends, stol'n forth of holy writ,
And seem a saint, when most I play the devil.†

But he is too deep a hypocrite to expose himself to discovery, by an affectation over-done: he does not quote, he only alludes to Scripture·

---

* Richard III. Act V. sc. 5.   † Ibid. Act I. sc. 4.

and assumes a general meekness of behaviour, without pretending to more religion or greater austerity than others. He claims credit only for the simplicity of his manners, when he says,

> Cannot a plain man live and think no harm,
> But thus his simple truth must be abus'd? *

His pious concern for his brother,

> Poor Clarence did forsake his father Warwick,
> Aye, and forswore himself; which Jesu pardon !†

is expressed without the least ostentation. His profession,

> 'Tis death to me to be at enmity;
> I hate it, and desire all good men's love ! ‡

is in the same unaffected strain: and his subsequent threat against those whom he charges with procuring the death of Clarence, that

> God will revenge it,§——

---

* Richard III. Act I. sc. 3.　　† Ibid. Act I. sc. 4.
‡ Ibid. Act II. sc. 1.　　§ Ibid.

is natural and becoming upon such a supposed provocation. Even when he puts on an extraordinary show of devotion, to impose upon the Lord Mayor and citizens, he affects to make no merit of it, when in their presence he says to Buckingham,

> I rather do beseech you to pardon me,
> Who, earnest in the service of my God,
> Deferr'd the visitation of my friends.
> But, leaving this, what is your Grace's pleasure? *

An hypocrisy so refined is not easily seen through; and in him it is the less suspected, on account of that frankness to which he is often prompted by his high courage, and into which he is sometimes hurried by the impetuosity of his temper. He is besides so complete a master of dissimulation, that his own account of himself is,

> ——I can smile, and murder while I smile;
> And cry content to that which grieves my heart;
> And wet my cheeks with artificial tears;
> And frame my face to all occasions.†

---

* Richard III. Act III. sc. 7.   † 3 Henry VI. Act III. sc. 3.

With such arts, it is not at all surprising that he for some time could conceal his character, and that he is never suspected of the mischief he intends, till it is executed; for his barbarity towards the House of Lancaster gave no warning: the animosities were mutual: cruelty was common to both sides, and was not therefore imputed to the men, but to the times. Richard is never reproached with it, except by the Lancastrian party; nor, till his own family feel it, is he reckoned more savage than the rest. Clarence, and the children of Clarence, trust to his goodness. His artifices impose upon others so much, that Lord Hastings observes of him,

> I think there's ne'er a man in Christendom
> Can lesser hide his love or hate than he;
> For by his face straight will you know his heart.*

His mother alone sees through his hypocrisy, and laments,

> ——That deceit should steal such gentle shape,
> And with a virtuous vizor hide deep vice!†

---

* Richard III. Act III. sc. 5. † Ibid. Act II. sc. 4.

And yet, when she reproaches him, that

> A grievous burden was thy birth to me;
> Tetchy and wayward was thy infancy;
> Thy school-days frightful, desp'rate, wild, and furious;
> Thy prime of manhood daring, bold, and vent'rous;
> Thy age confirm'd, proud, subtle, sly, and bloody,[*]

she acknowledges that she had seen only into the frowardness and violence of his temper, but knew not of the wickedness of his heart till his prime of manhood was past; so long and so artfully had he concealed his disposition! But when the measure of his iniquities is filled by the murder of his infant nephews, he from that time drops all hypocrisy; which, after so atrocious a deed, could not deceive; and which, having served his principal purpose, he had occasion for no longer.

But Macbeth wants no disguise of his natural disposition, for it is not bad; he does not affect

---

[*] Richard III. Act IV. sc. 6.

more piety than he has: on the contrary, a part of his distress arises from a real sense of religion; which, in the passages already quoted, makes him regret that he could not join with the chamberlains in prayer for God's blessing; and bewail that he has *given his eternal jewel to the common enemy of man.* He continually reproaches himself for his deeds; no use can harden him; confidence cannot silence, and even despair cannot stifle the cries of his conscience. By the first murder he committed he *put rancours in the vessel of his peace;* and of the last he owns to Macduff,

————my soul is too much charg'd
With blood of thine already.*————

How heavily it was charged with his crimes, appears from his asking the physician,

Canst thou not minister to a mind diseas'd,
Pluck from the memory a rooted sorrow,
Raze out the written troubles of the brain,

---

* Macbeth, Act V. sc. 7.

And, with some sweet oblivious antidote,
Cleanse the stuff'd bosom of that perilous stuff,
Which weighs upon the heart?*

For though it is the disorder of Lady Macbeth, that gives occasion to these questions, yet the feeling with which he describes the sensations he wishes to be removed; the longing he expresses for the means of doing it; the plaintive measure of the lines; and the rage into which he bursts, when he says,

Throw physic to the dogs, I'll none of it;†

upon being told that

———therein the patient
Must minister unto himself; ‡———

evidently show, that, in his own mind, he is all the while making the application to himself. His credulity in the mysterious assurances of safety, which the incantations of the witches had

---

* Macbeth, Act V. sc. 3.   † Ibid.
‡ Ibid. Act III. sc. 5.

procured, proceeds from superstition. He considers those who give him such assurances as

>——spirits that know
>All mortal consequences:*——

and yet he condemns all intercourse with them, at the very time that he seeks it; and he calls his own application to the sisters a resolution

>——to know,
>By the worst means, the worst.†——

Conscious, therefore, of all these feelings, he has no occasion to assume the appearance, but is obliged to conceal the force of them: and Lady Macbeth finds it necessary more than once to suggest to him the precautions proper to hide the agitations of his mind. After the murder of Duncan, she bids him,

>Get on your night-gown, lest occasion call us,
>And show us to be watchers. Be not lost
>So poorly in your thoughts.‡——

---

* Macbeth, Act V. sc. 3. † Ibid. Act III. sc. 5.
‡ Ibid. Act II. sc. 3.

and while he is meditating the death of Banquo, she says to him,

> Come on;——
> Gentle my lord, sleek o'er your rugged looks;
> Be bright and jovial with your friends to-night.*

Which kind of disguise is all that is wanting to him: and yet, when he had assumed it, he in both instances betrays himself: in the first, by his too guarded conversation with Macduff and Lenox, which has been quoted already; and in the last, by an over-acted regard for Banquo, of whose absence from the feast he affects to complain, that he may not be suspected of knowing the cause of it, though at the same time he very unguardedly drops an allusion to that cause, when he says,

> Here had we now our country's honour roof'd,
> Were the grac'd person of our Banquo present;
> Whom may I rather challenge for unkindness,
> Than pity for mischance! †——

---

* Macbeth, Act III. sc. 3.   † Ibid. Act III. sc. 5.

This he says before the ghost rises; and after it is vanished, he, from the same consciousness, reassumes the same affectation; and, as soon as he is recovered, drinks

> ——to the general joy of the whole table;
> And to our dear friend Banquo, whom we miss;
> Would he were here!*——

Richard is able to put on a general character, directly the reverse of his disposition; and it is ready to him upon every occasion. But Macbeth cannot effectually conceal his sensations, when it is most necessary to conceal them; nor act a part which does not belong to him with any degree of consistency; and the same weakness of mind, which disqualifies him from maintaining such a force upon his nature, shows itself still further in that hesitation and dulness to dare, which he feels in himself, and allows in others. His whole proceeding in his treason

---

* Macbeth, Act III. sc. 5.

against Duncan is full of it; of which the references already made to his behaviour then are sufficient proofs. Against Banquo he acts with more determination, for the reasons which have been given: and yet he most unnecessarily acquaints the murderers with the reasons of his conduct; and even informs them of the behaviour he proposes to observe afterwards, by saying to them,

> ——though I could
> With barefac'd power sweep him from my sight,
> And bid my will avouch it, yet I must not,
> For certain friends that are both his and mine,
> Whose loves I may not drop; but wail his fate,
> Whom I myself struck down:*——

which particularity and explanation to men who did not desire it; the confidence he places in those who could only abuse it; and the very needless caution of secrecy implied in this

---

* Macbeth, Act III. sc. 2.

speech, are so many symptoms of a feeble mind; which again appears, when, after they had undertaken the business, he bids them

——resolve themselves apart;*

and thereby leaves them an opportunity to retract, if they had not been more determined than he is, who supposes time to be requisite for settling such resolutions. His sending a third murderer to join the others, just at the moment of action, and without any notice, is a further proof of the same imbecility; and that so glaring as to strike them, who observe upon it, that

> He needs not our mistrust, since he delivers
> Our offices, and what we have to do,
> To the direction just.†

Richard, always determined, and taking his determination himself, never waits to be incited,

---

* Macbeth, Act III. sc. 2. † Ibid. Act III. sc. 4.

nor ever idly accounts for his conduct; but fixed to his purpose, makes other men only his instruments, not his confidents or advisers. Even Buckingham is no more; he discards him as soon as he pretends to have any judgment of his own; and assigns for his reason, that

> ———none are for me
> That look into me with considerate eyes:
> High-reaching Buckingham grows circumspect.*

And again,

> The deep-revolving, witty Buckingham
> No more shall be the neighbour to my counsels.†

He had

> ———learn'd that fearful commenting
> Is leaden servitor to dull delay;
> Delay leads impotent and snail-pac'd beggary.
> Then, fiery expedition! be my wing,
> Jove's Mercury, and herald for a king!‡

Prompt in decision, he does not hesitate upon collateral circumstances, but attends to the

---

* Richard III. Act IV. sc. 2. † Ibid. ‡ Ibid. sc. 3.

principal, point only, and resolves upon it instantly, though it be the doom of death which he pronounces. Shakespere, who had such variety of phrase at command, does not repeat the same without a design. An example has already been given of a particular meaning conveyed by the frequent use which Macbeth makes of the same terms, in asserting his pretensions to the character of manliness. Another instance, of the like kind, is the repetition by Richard, of the same words, *off with his head!* upon three or four different occasions. The readiness and the certainty of his resolutions are expressed by them; and yet, unrelenting as he is in all such bloody deeds, which seem necessary to his purpose, he is easily diverted from them, if a greater object presents itself: as upon the defection of Lord Stanley, and after having pronounced the sentence,

  Off with his son George's head![*]

---

[*] Richard III. Act V. sc. 7.

he readily acquiesces in the representation of the Duke of Norfolk,

> My lord, the enemy is past the marsh;
> After the battle let George Stanley die :*

to which he makes no reply; but immediately swelling with ardour, and feeling

> A thousand hearts beat great within his bosom,†

he rushes with exultation to the field. In the same manner he is without difficulty withheld from killing Queen Margaret, upon the greater idea arising of murdering King Henry; though at the moment he was chaffed by her taunts, and flushed with the blood of her son: but he no sooner conceives that design, than big with the thought, he suffers the slightest interposition to check his impetuosity, and makes even his vengeance give way. Macbeth, on the contrary, is irresolute in his counsels, and

---

* Richard III. Act V. sc. 7. † Ibid.

languid in the execution; he cannot look steadily at his principal object, but dwells upon circumstances, and always does too much or too little. Besides the proofs which have been given of these weaknesses in his character, through the whole conduct of his designs against Duncan and Banquo, another may be drawn from his attempt upon Macduff; whom he first sends for, without acquainting Lady Macbeth with his intention; then betrays the secret, by asking of her, after the company are risen from the banquet,

Macb. How say'st thou, that Macduff denies his person
At our great bidding?
Lady. Did you send to him, Sir?
Macb. I hear it by the way; but I will send.*

The time of making this inquiry, when it has no relation to what had just passed, otherwise than as his apprehensions might connect it; the

---

* Macbeth, Act III. sc. 5.

addressing of the question to her, who, as appears from what she says, knew nothing of the matter; and his awkward attempt then to disguise it, are strong evidences of the disorder of his mind. He had not yet formed his resolution; he delays till he has consulted the witches; their enigmatical answers make him doubt more: but his fear determines him on the death of Macduff, who, during this procrastination, escapes into England. Macbeth no sooner hears of his flight, than he is sensible of his own weakness; and, rushing into the contrary extreme, he vents his rage for the disappointment, impotently and needlessly, on the family of the fugitive, who were not at all the objects of his jealousy; crying out,

> Time, thou anticipat'st my dread exploits;
> The flighty purpose never is o'ertook,
> Unless the deed go with it. From this moment,
> The very firstlings of my heart shall be
> The firstlings of my hand. And even now,
> To crown my thoughts with acts, be it thought and done:

> The castle of Macduff I will surprise,
> Seize upon Fife, give to the edge o' th' sword
> His wife, his babe, and all unfortunate souls
> That trace him to his line. No boasting like a fool;
> This deed I'll do before the purpose cool.*

Thus agitated always by his fears or his fury, he ravages his kingdom with a boundless waste of cruelty till

> ——the dead man's knell
> Was there scarce ask'd, for whom? and good men's lives
> Expir'd before the flowers in their caps,
> Dying or ere they sicken'd.†——

While Richard, though he has less remorse and less humanity, yet because he acts upon design not from passion, stops when his purpose is accomplished; he destroys without pity, not without occasion; and directs, but does not let loose his tyranny.

A mind so framed and so tortured as that of Macbeth, when the hour of extremity presses

---

* Macbeth, Act IV. sc. 2. † Ibid. sc. 5.

upon him, can find no refuge but in despair; and the expression of that despair by Shakespere is perhaps one of the finest pictures that ever was exhibited. It is wildness, inconsistency, and disorder, to such a degree, and so apparent, that

> Some say he's mad; others, who lesser hate him,
> Do call it valiant fury: but for certain,
> He cannot buckle his distemper'd cause
> Within the belt of rule.*——

It is presumption without hope, and confidence without courage: that confidence rests upon his superstition; he buoys himself up with it against all the dangers that threaten him, and yet sinks upon every fresh alarm:

> Bring me no more reports; let them fly all:
> Till Birnam wood remove to Dunsinane,
> I cannot taint with fear. What's the boy Malcolm?
> Was he not born of woman? Spirits, that know
> All mortal consequences, have pronounc'd it,

---

* Macbeth, Act V. sc. 2.

> *Fear not, Macbeth! no man that's born of woman*
> *Shall e'er have power upon thee.*—Fly, false Thanes,
> And mingle with the English Epicures!
> The mind I sway by, and the heart I bear,
> Shall never sagg with doubt, nor shake with fear!*

His faith in these assurances is implicit; he really is persuaded that he may defy the forces of his enemies, and the treachery of his friends; but immediately after, only on seeing a man who, not having the same support, is frightened at the numbers approaching against them, he catches his apprehensions; tells him,

> ——those linen cheeks of thine
> Are counsellors to fear;†——

and then, though nothing had happened to impeach the credit of those assurances on which he relied, he gives way to the depression of his spirits, and desponds in the midst of security:

---

* Macbeth, Act V. sc. 3. † Ibid.

> Take thy face hence.—Seyton! I'm sick at heart,
> When I behold——Seyton! I say, this push
> Will cheer me ever, or disease me now.
> I have liv'd long enough; my way of life
> Is fallen into the sear, the yellow leaf.*

By these reflections, by those which follow on his uncomfortable prospect of old age, and by those which he afterwards makes on the vanity of life, when he hears that Lady Macbeth is no more, he appears to be preparing for his fate. But his seeming composure is not resignation: it is passion still; it is one of the irregularities of despair, which sometimes overwhelms him, at other times starts into rage, and is at all times intemperate and extravagant. The resolution, with which he bore up against the desertion of the Thanes, fails him, upon meeting the messenger who comes to tell him the numbers of the enemy: when he receives the

---

* Macbeth, Act V. sc. 3.

confirmation of that news, his dejection turns into fury, and he declares,

> I'll fight, till from my bones my flesh is hack'd.*

He then impetuously gives his orders, to

> Send out more horses; skirr the country round;
> Hang those that talk of fear.†──

He repeats them afterwards with impatience. Though the enemy is still at a distance, he calls for his armour; notwithstanding Seyton's remonstrance, that *it is not needed yet*, he persists in putting it on; he calls for it again eagerly afterwards; he bids the person who is assisting him *dispatch;* then, the moment it is on, he pulls it off again, and directs his attendants *to bring it after him.* In the midst of all this violence and hurry, the melancholy which preys upon him shews itself by the sympathy he expresses so feelingly when the diseased mind of

---

* Macbeth, Act V. sc. 3.   † Ibid.

Lady Macbeth is mentioned; and yet neither the troubles of his conscience, nor his concern for her, can divert his attention from the distress of his situation. He tells her physician, that *the Thanes fly from him;* and betrays to him, whose assistance he could not want, and in whom he did not mean to place any particular confidence, his apprehensions of the English forces. After he has forbid those about him to bring him in any more reports, he anxiously inquires for news; he dreads every danger which he supposes he scorns; at last he recurs to his superstition, as to the only relief from his agony; and concludes the agitated scene, as he had begun it, with declaring that he

——will not be afraid of death or bane,
Till Birnam forest come to Dusinane.*

At his next appearance, he gives his orders, and

---

* Macbeth, Act V. sc. 3.

considers his situation more calmly; but still there is no spirit in him. If he is for a short time sedate, it is because

> ———he has surfeited with horrors;
> Direness, familiar to his slaughterous thoughts,
> Cannot now start him.*———

He appears composed, only because he is become almost indifferent to every thing: he is hardly affected by the death of the Queen, whom he tenderly loved: he checks himself for wishing she had lived longer; for he is weary himself of life, which in his estimation now

> Is but a walking shadow; a poor player,
> That struts and frets his hour upon the stage,
> And then is heard no more: it is a tale
> Told by an idiot, full of sound and fury,
> Signifying nothing.†

Yet though he grows more careless about his

---

* Macbeth, Act V. sc. 5.   † Ibid.

fate, he cannot reconcile himself to it; he still flatters himself that he shall escape, even after he has found *the equivocation of the fiend.* When Birnam wood appeared to come towards Dunsinane, he trusts to the other assurance; and believes that he

>——bears a charmed life, which must not yield
>To one of woman born.*————

His confidence however begins to fail him; he raves as soon as he perceives that he has reason to doubt of the promises which had been made to him, and says,

>If this which he avouches does appear,
>There is no flying hence, nor tarrying here.
>I 'gin to be a-weary of the sun,
>And wish the state o' th' world were now undone.—
>Ring the alarum bell:—blow, wind! come, wrack!
>At least we'll die with harness on our back.†

---

* Macbeth, Act V. sc. 5.   † Ibid.

But sensible, at last, that he is driven to extremity, and that

> They've tied him to a stake; he cannot fly,
> But, bear-like, he must fight the course,[*]

he summons all his fortitude; and agreeably to the manliness of character to which he had always formed himself, behaves with more temper and spirit during the battle than he had before. He is so well recovered from the disorder he had been in, that the natural sensibility of his disposition finds even in the field an opportunity to work; where he declines to fight with Macduff, not from fear, but from a consciousness of the wrongs he had done to him: he therefore answers his provoking challenge, only by saying,

> Of all men else I have avoided thee:
> But get thee back; my soul is too much charged
> With blood of thine already;[†]——

---

[*] Macbeth, Act V. sc. 6. [†] Ibid. sc. 7.

and then patiently endeavours to persuade this injured adversary to desist from so unequal a combat; for he is confident that it must be fatal to Macduff, and therefore tells him,

> ——Thou losest labour:
> As easy may'st thou the intrenchant air
> With thy keen sword impress, as make me bleed:
> Let fall thy blade on vulnerable crests:
> I bear a charmed life.*——

But his reliance on this charm being taken away by the explanation given by Macduff, and every hope now failing him, though he wishes not to fight, yet his sense of honour being touched by the threat, to be made *the shew and gaze of the time*, and all his passions being now lost in despair, his habits recur to govern him; he disdains the thought of disgrace, and dies as becomes a soldier. His last words are,

---

* Macbeth, Act V. sc. 7.

>   ——I will not yield,
> To kiss the ground before young Malcolm's feet,
> And to be baited by the rabble's curse.
> Tho' Birnam wood be come to Dunsinane,
> And thou oppos'd, being of no woman born,
> Yet I will try the last. Before my body
> I throw my warlike shield: lay on, Macduff!
> And damn'd be he that first cries, *Hold! enough.*[*]

If this behaviour of Macbeth required, it would receive illustration, by comparing it with that of Richard in circumstances not very different. When he is to fight for his crown and for his life, he prepares for the crisis with the most perfect evenness of temper; and rises, as the danger thickens, into ardour, without once starting out into intemperance, or ever sinking into dejection. Though he is so far from being supported, that he is depressed, as much as a brave spirit can be depressed, by supernatural means, and, instead of having a superstitious confidence, is threatened by all the ghosts of all whom he

---

[*] Macbeth, Act V. sc. 7.

has murdered, that they will *sit heavy on his soul to-morrow*, yet he soon shakes off the impression they had made, and is again as gallant as ever. Before their appearance he feels a presentiment of his fate; he observes that he

> ——has not that alacrity of spirit,
> Nor cheer of mind, that he was wont to have;*

and upon signifying his intention of laying in Bosworth field that night, the reflection of *where to-morrow?* occurs to him; but he pushes it aside by answering, *Well, all's one for that:* and he struggles against the lowness of spirits which he feels, but cannot account for, by calling for a bowl of wine, and applying to business. Instead of giving way to it in himself, he attends to every symptom of dejection in others, and endeavours to dispel them. He asks,

> My lord of Surry, why look you so sad?†

---

* Richard III. Act V. sc. 3.   † Ibid.

He inquires,

> Saw'st thou the melancholy lord Northumberland?*

and *is satisfied* upon being told, that he and Surry were busied in *cheering up the soldiers*. He adverts to every circumstance which can dishearten or encourage his attendants or his troops, and observes upon them accordingly. When he perceives the gloominess of the morning, and that the sun might probably not be seen that day, his observation is,

> Not shine to-day? why, what is that to me
> More than to Richmond? for the self-same heaven,
> That frowns on me, looks sadly upon him.†

He takes notice of the superiority of his numbers; he points out the circumstance, that

> ——the king's name is a tower of strength,
> Which they upon the adverse faction want.‡

He represents the enemy as a troop only of

---

* Richard III. Act V. sc. 3.   † Ibid. sc. 7.   ‎ibid. sc. 3.

banditti; he urges the inexperience of Richmond; and he animates his soldiers with their

> ancient word of courage, fair St. George;*

the effect of which he had before intimated to the Duke of Norfolk; when, having explained to him the disposition he intended, he asks him,

> This, and St. George to boot! what think'st thou, Norfolk?†

He deliberately, and after having *surveyed the vantage of the ground*, forms that disposition by himself; for which purpose he calls for ink and paper, and being informed that it is ready, directs his guard to watch, and his attendants to leave him; but before he retires, he issues the necessary orders. They are not, like those of Macbeth, general and violent, but temperate and particular; delivered coolly, and distinctly

---

* Richard III. Act V. sc. 7.   † Ibid.

given to different persons. To the Duke of Norfolk he trusts the mounting of the guard during the night, and bids him be ready himself early in the morning. He directs Catesby to

> Send out a pursuivant at arms
> To Stanley's regiment; bid him bring his power
> Before sun-rising.*

He bids his menial servants,

> Saddle White Surry for the field to-morrow;
> Look that my staves be sound, and not too heavy.†

And, instead of hastily putting on, and as hastily pulling off his armour, he quietly asks,

> What, is my beaver easier than it was?
> And all my armour laid into my tent?‡

directing them to come about midnight to help to arm him. He is attentive to every circumstance preparatory to the battle; and preserves throughout a calmness and presence of

---

* Richard III. Act V. sc. 3. † Ibid. ‡ Ibid.

mind, which denote his intrepidity. He does not lose it upon being told, that *the foe vaunts in the field;* but recollecting the orders he had given over-night, now calls for the execution of them, by directing Lord Stanley to be sent for, and his own horse to be caparisoned. He tells the Duke of Norfolk, who is next in command to himself, the disposition he had formed; and every thing being in readiness, he then makes a speech to encourage his soldiers: but on hearing the enemy's drum, he concludes with,

> Fight, gentlemen of England! fight, bold yeomen!
> Draw, archers, draw your arrows to the head!
> Spur your proud horses hard, and ride in blood;
> Amaze the welkin with your broken staves![*]

But even in this sally of ardour he is not hurried away by a blind impetuosity, but still gives orders, and distinguishes the persons to whom he addresses them. From this moment

---

[*] Richard III. Act V. sc. 7.

he is all on fire; and possessed entirely with the great objects around him, others of lesser note are below his attention. Swelling himself with courage, and inspiring his troops with confidence of victory, he rushes on the enemy. It is not a formed sense of honour, nor a cold fear of disgrace, which impels him to fight; but a natural high spirit, and bravery exulting in danger: and being sensible that the competition is only personal between him and Richmond, he directs all his efforts to the destruction of his rival; endeavours himself to single him out; and, *seeking him in the throat of death, he sets his own life upon the cast.* Five times foiled in his aim, unhorsed, and surrounded with foes, he still persists *to stand the hazard of the die;* and, having *enacted more wonders than a man,* loses his life in an attempt so worthy of himself.

Thus, from the beginning of their history to their last moments, are the characters of

Macbeth and Richard preserved entire and distinct: and though probably Shakespere, when he was drawing the one, had no attention to the other; yet as he conceived them to be widely different, expressed his conceptions exactly, and copied both from nature, they necessarily became contrasts to each other; and, by seeing them together, that contrast is more apparent, especially where the comparison is not between opposite qualities, but arises from the different degrees, or from a particular display, or total omission, of the same quality. This last must often happen, as the character of Macbeth is much more complicated than that of Richard; and therefore, when they are set in opposition, the judgment of the poet shews itself as much in what he has left out of the latter, as in what he has inserted. The picture of Macbeth is also, for the same reason, much the more highly finished of the two; for it required a greater variety, and a greater delicacy of painting, to express and to blend with consistency all the several properties which are ascribed to him. That of Richard is marked by more careless strokes, but they are, notwithstanding, perfectly just. Much bad composition may indeed be found in the part; it is a fault from which the best of Shakespere's Plays are not exempt, and with which this Play particularly abounds; and the taste of the age in which he wrote, though it may afford some excuse, yet cannot entirely vindicate the exceptionable passages. After every reasonable allowance, they must still remain blemishes ever to be lamented; but happily, for the most part, they only obscure, they do not disfigure his draughts from nature. Through whole speeches and scenes character is often wanting; but in the worst instances of this kind Shakespere is but insipid; he is not inconsistent; and in his peculiar excellence of drawing characters, though he often neglects to exert his talents, he is very rarely guilty of perverting them.

APPENDIX.

EXTRACT I.

The principal merit of Sir Walter Scott, as it is of Shakespere, (whom he strongly resembles both in his excellences and his defects,) is always the variety and individuality of his *characters*.

This last expression may perhaps require some explanation; especially since Dr. Johnson has made it a part of Shakespere's praise, that "in the writings of other poets a character is too often an individual; in those of Shakespere it is commonly a species." We do not understand the first part of this sentence. We even doubt whether Dr. Johnson himself attached to it a precise meaning. The human mind seems unable to imagine any thing perfectly new: all it can do is to vary the combinations of what it has known. The wildest heraldic monsters are formed of parts of existing animals: the Chimæra herself was Προσθε Λεων, οπιθεν δε Δρακων. So in the moral world, we can imagine only those faculties, passions, and habits, which we can have known from observation or reflection. Of these three great divisions of the human mind, the same *faculties* and the same *passions* belong, though in different degrees, to every individual; but the *habits* of men are infinitely diversified; and it is by the variety of their habits, and the comparative force of their faculties and passions, that men differ from one another; and according to these diversities they are classed. Thus men are called servile or independent, covetous or prodigal, tellers of truth or falsehood, according to their *habits;* bold or timid, irritable or phlegmatic, according to their *passions;* and acute or dull, rapid or slow, clear-headed or confused, according to their *faculties.* Each class may be said to form a different moral species; but as the different classes are all *cross-divisions,* the same person, according to the many points of view in which he may be considered, belongs to as many different species: and from the innumerable modes in which those different characteristics may be combined, results the infinite variety of human character. But to draw a full moral and intellectual portrait of even a single individual, would be impossible. Inferior writers content themselves with giving to each character a superabundance of one or two habits, faculties, or passions. They make their kings proud, and their warriors brave, and are satisfied. Such a character is strictly not an individual, but a species. It is logically consituted of a genus and a differentia. But such are not the characters of real life. Nature proceeds not by abstraction but by concretion. We know that every individual with whom we have been acquainted, has differed in innumerable points from every other individual; and we recognise the truth of those fictitious characters only which have also their distinguishing peculiarities, and which may be referred, according to the point in which we are for the time considering them, to one or other of many different species. This appears to us to be the great merit of Shakespere; and this is also the merit of our author.

To take our examples from the novel we are now reviewing, he has given to Joshua Geddes, intrepid courage, a hasty temper, and firmness of purpose approaching to obstinacy. Such might have been the qualities of a freebooter: but he has added a benevolent disposition, and religious scruples against the resistance of injury. He is indifferent to personal show, but his simplicity is qualified by a taste for the beauties of nature in their ornamented state. His exterior is unassuming, but his residence is adorned with expensive gardens and conservatories.

Peter Peebles is vain, litigious, hard-hearted, credulous, a liar, and a drunkard. An ordinary writer would have made six characters out of the qualities which Sir Walter has condensed into one. And how bold is the relief in which it stands out!

It is to be observed, too, that a character is in general both probable and interesting, in proportion to the *dissimilarity* of its different constituents, provided that they are not inconsistent. Partly from the novelty of the combination, and partly because the reader accounts for the union of qualities not suggested by one another, by fancying it a copy of an existing original. It is this combination that gives such vivacity to the character of Nanty Ewart. He is a smuggler, and, as might be expected, reckless and drunken. But he is also the son of a minister, and has retained of a learned education the fruits which such an education often produces: just enough recollection of his Latin to make him a pedant, and of his religion to make him hate a Catholic.—*London Review, No.* 1, *page* 28. *Redgauntlet.*

EXTRACT II.

The man[*] who, without rank or fortune, could for thirty or forty years set all law at defiance, who though peculiarly obnoxious to the government, not merely as breaking its laws and plundering its subjects, but as a rebel and a traitor, and at deadly feud with the great men on whose property he lived, could resist all their power, and elude all their stratagems, without being overwhelmed by superior force, or betrayed by the treachery of his own companions—taken, as many of them must have been, from among the least trustworthy of men —must have been a man of extraordinary talents, and, mixed

---

[*] Rob Roy.

with his great vices, of extraordinary virtues. He must have had the first in order to play his own part well; the second in order to retain in devoted fidelity his associates.

And he must have been a man of extraordinary *courage*. Some of our readers may perhaps be surprised at hearing that the last has been doubted; and, certainly, on the occasions which are the most usual tests of courage, he behaved ill. He fought two duels, and in both of them yielded almost immediately in no very honourable manner. And, at Sheriff Muir, on the only occasion in which, with the temporary command of the clan, he had an opportunity of showing at once his spirit and his devotion

> " He never advanced
> From the place he was stanced,
> Till nae mair was to do there at a' man."

But the fact is, that no two things can be more different than the courage of an outlaw and that of a soldier. The first is founded on familiarity with danger—it is the virtue of rude times, and can be obtained only by repeated exposure to peril. The second is founded on the point of honour—it can exist only in a most artificial state of society, and is so far from requiring repeated exposure, that it is often most perfectly exhibited by men who were never in danger before in their lives. The first arises from the contempt which is the proverbial result of familiarity. A man who has been often in danger has learnt to distinguish its real, from its apparent, symptoms—to fear the lightning, not the thunder. He has learnt to balance the hazards of different modes of escape—to wait the opportunity for putting in practice that which appears most promising, and to snatch that opportunity when, on the whole, it appears probable that a better will not offer. All this supposes great calmness and presence of mind, but is compatible with a thorough detestation of all unnecessary risk. It not only is compatible with such a detestation, but its natural tendency, if uncounteracted by other causes, must be to produce it. The constant association in such a man's mind with danger, has been, that it is a thing to be as much as possible avoided. His constant meditation has been, how shall I attain my object with the least hazard, and, having attained it, how shall I best provide for my safety? Such habits fit him admirably for avoiding danger, and for encountering it when it cannot be avoided; but very ill for thrusting himself into it when it can, or for continuing in it when any mode of escape is opened. No man can show more calmness in danger than a North American Indian, or try more frightful modes of escape, if they are the best that offer, or fight more desperately if he is absolutely forced to fight. But he will not fight *unless* he is forced. He will rather endure any fatigue, cold, sleeplessness, and famine, to surprise his deadliest enemy, than meet him on fair, or nearly fair, terms.

Military courage is founded on the glory attached to the endurance of danger, and to the infamy attached to undue fear. And, as no natural bounds can be assigned to qualities, which are in themselves unnatural, the necessary endurance was first raised to insensibility, and at last, to delight in danger. In that most artificial period which followed both the English and French civil wars, when the minds of men, deprived of the violent sources of excitement to which they had been accustomed, ran into every sort of affectation and absurdity, a gentleman seems to have been bound to hold any opportunity of encountering danger a source of unalloyed enjoyment. Any ulterior purpose, however frivolous, was not to be required. A man who was so fortunate as to receive, or to have a fair opportunity of giving, a challenge, had the patronage of inviting three or four friends to partake in the amusement; and while the principals, who might be supposed to have some object in it, were fighting, the seconds, instead of minding their duty as umpires, fought too, to shew how much they enjoyed a chance of being wounded or killed. The story is well known of the man who offered Lord Stair such an opportunity, provided he would exercise this patronage in his favour; and who refused to interfere further, when he found he could derive no advantage from the transaction, as his lordship's list was full for his next three affairs. The story is probably coloured, but it shows what were the feelings, at least the cant, of the times in which it could be circulated. A man so trained would have shone on those occasions, on which we have described Rob Roy as failing; but it may be questioned whether he would have heard with the same presence of mind, the Baillie's steps on the Tolbooth's stairs; and whether, if strapped, like him, to Evan Bigg, he would have had sufficient boldness to plan his escape, sufficient composure to execute it, or sufficient patience to delay it to the most favourable instant.—*Quarterly Review, No. 50, page* 112. *Rob Roy, &c.*

EXTRACT III.

The general inferiority which we have ascribed to the plot,* does not extend to the characters. It is difficult to select where there is so much general excellence, but on the whole we prefer Conachar. His character is perfectly tragic, neither too bad for sympathy, nor so good as to render his calamity revolting; but its great merit is the boldness with which we are called upon to sympathise with a deficiency which is generally the subject of unmitigated scorn. It is impossible not to feel the deepest commiseration for a youth cursed by nature with extreme sensibility both to *shame* and *fear*, suddenly raised from a life of obscurity and peace, to head a confederacy of warlike savages, and forced immediately afterwards to elect, before the eyes of

---

* Fair Maid of Perth.